ABOUT THE AUTHOR

Claire Trévien was born in Brittany. Her pamphlet *Low-Tide Lottery* was published by Salt in 2011. She is the editor of Sabotage Reviews. Her first collection, *The Shipwrecked House* (Penned in the Margins, 2013), was longlisted for the Guardian First Book Award and subsequently transformed for the stage.

ALSO BY CLAIRE TRÉVIEN

Astéronymes
Claire Trévien

Penned in the Margins

LONDON

PUBLISHED BY PENNED IN THE MARGINS
Toynbee Studios, 28 Commercial Street, London E1 6AB
www.pennedinthemargins.co.uk

First published 2016

Printed in the United Kingdom by TJ International

ISBN
978-1-908058348

ACKNOWLEDGEMENTS

With thanks to the editors of *Antiphon, Best Friends Forever: Poems on Female Friendship, Bone Bouquet, The Emma Press Anthology of the Sea, Fake Poems, The Learned Pig, Long Poem Magazine, POETRY* and *Furies: a Poetry Anthology of Women Warriors*, where some of these poems were first published. Several of these poems were created after a Clipperton Project residency to the northern isles in August 2015. 'You' was commissioned by the Mathematical Institute, Oxford, as part of the exhibition *Illegitimate Objects*.

I would like to thank the following people for supporting my trip to the northern isles (in no particular order): Emily Hasler, Sam Loveless, Natalie Newman, David Hirons, Lucy Ayrton, Steve Nash, James Webster, Tom Claydon, Claire Sheridan, Martha Greengrass, Paul Martin, Tania Hershman, Linda Goulden, Robert Harper, Michael Symons Roberts, Adam Horovitz, Jo Bell, Dominic Conlon, Adriana Jacobs, Ruth Stacey, Jenna Gregg, Patricia Stoughton, A.F. Harrold, Gerry Cambridge, Clare Mosley, Kiran Millwood-Hargrave, Ian Chung, Rishi Dastidar.

I would like to thank two early readers of the manuscript, Harry Giles and Gareth Prior, whose insights, whilst not always applied, were immensely valuable. Thanks to Alex Boyd, too, who guided me through Arran and accidentally triggered this collection.

CONTENTS

To past, present and future friends

Astéronymes

The Evening After

After James Merrill

We spent one evening, tired of games and each other,
watching our reflections on a screen —
four in a two-seater, angling like sardines.
For a dog's hair I'd milked the wine, uttered
words like "that's the cure!", swivelled
the puckering glass like a mock-dandy,
blood slushing at my temples, until the spill,
a fatal expression on the white and navy,
ruined the smoothness past salvation. A cough
of salt, the patting of the fabric, perhaps enough.

The Museum of Water

I never tire of the repetition of bottles:
the evaporation of grief,
a great silty presence,
a shallow song.

Here is a bath bomb tuned to your body.
Elsewhere, backwash, broken water,
a hacked freezer, your favourite river
carried from one country to another.

Light in this postcard is
sieved through a kidney.
There is too much demand
for a street.

I'm naturally still. A pearl
starts with an attack
shattering the shell.

I splinter the pause,
reach for the bowl
and pour out voices
improbably fractured.

Instructions for Making a Standing Stone

Steep a stone into rain, or a bucket of sand.
Fresh-gathered stones should be bruised by
stamping barks into their skin. Understand
that, properly dried, they may last indefinitely.

Strengthen the core with chunks of teeth
and lichen grated through joints. If too
stocky, plant it uphill; the right brand
of wind will slim it down with time, to
stoop over the moors — a cracked wand.

Confirmation Bias

Kervadol Dolmen

Raking in signs of early life: collapsed
arks, kicked in the groin. Sponged soil
swallows the spineless; rain faxes
the dead long after we don't. Shoaled

history, you're slumped waiting for
the grass to dry — ravaged raw slabs
with corridor breath. Eyes uncorked;
a four-legged beast, a table without seats.

Crab-crouched crates, not sure why you wait
as a huddle — the secret to eternal youth
is to be singular. I count the spots where suede
puckers, where your mouth's left unzipped.

Rollright Stones

Like shaking hands with a ghost
AUBREY BURL, THE STONE CIRCLES OF BRITAIN, IRELAND, AND BRITTANY

Men come and stand in its centre —
    stubbled, pocked, and pickled —
and interrupt my poem
    about unknowable history. I choose a spot
where they're out of sight.

    They say that each time you blink
a stone will hide behind another
    — the men cut
and paste, becoming slighter.
    Their arms are full of peepholes.

I've been whispering with my men.
    We've touched
time's buzzcut,
    swallowed a tree,
become stone.

    There's a spectator in my boot

that refuses to own up.
　　　You know,
the grass here is the kind of green
　　　that can only exist after rain
or a monitor failure.

Expiry Date

for Richard Fortey

Some places rehearse the same
landscape over and over / Stromatolites
timehop to the Precambrian / I scroll
through the same living skin
find your comments ossified / We used to think
the earth was as old as a cooling-off period
but I've changed my mind / Other architectures
have rusted under the sun / Their to-do lists
last for centuries / Tracks are left for the next
caretaker / Not much is known
as to how the mug grew
on the placemat / Everything I do
is sulphur-stained / Life grows
in extremes / I share this memory
with you /

You

shaken skyscraper, dried octopus, cornered grape,
shifting footnote, anemone shower, rusty cape.

Shored away, you've been plastered with tape
shunned and domesticated. Your patterns escape

sharply — incomprehensible rhythms, and I drape
shoddily over you, hands all over the pastries, nape

shipping through the cloth, wine into crowdscape,
shoes sprouting strings, limbs stiffening into crape

sheets and then smothered, not quite, not ever, agape.

Self-Portrait in the Body of a Dolmen

After Frances Justine Post

i

We come upon it,
          smelling like a thousand hands.
I crawl into the well-tongued path.

The heart,
          a lump of granite, heaves.
You ring its veins.

I lie in its ribcage
          as rain rushes up.
Each wave deepens the soil.

You've left,
          back to the car perhaps;
I squint but can only see green.

ii

Skyprinted rocks. Fern-
typoed legs, green pimpled
over its jamb.

Naturally, it has an ego.

Ever hairy, yet sewn
shut, that's Time:
a web that yawns.

Networking

The city shakes my jaw loose,
until the teeth forget they ever met.
Talking becomes a juggle.
Skin falls

in potato peels. I collage limbs as
best I can — reconfigure the meaning
of mind: does it fit in the finger tips
or winter

in the knee cap? My ankle vanishes
in the sinkhole. I replace it with a photocopy,
a taped-up ghost. I hear chewing gum can
hold the springs

of a car engine together. My pylon
elbows are collapsing, propped up
by wires. Limestone joints: the first
sign of Summer.

Araucaria Araucana

The monkey's despair
with its daggered leaves.

A staircase of fins
erupting from soil.

A feral pudding
pocketed by Archie

at a dinner party
and raised on the deck
like a parrot.

A living fossil
with multiple fake IDs.

An alcoholic monument

easier to intoxicate
than your average statue.

The Museum of Author Corrections

that summer, my <u>bedroom knew</u>   How does it know? Is it sentient?

    it had <u>**grown far older**</u>   By how much exactly?

its walls flickered with <u>archival footage</u>   Oh I've heard of that gadget.

    I let my body grow

heavy with <u>peat</u>   This reminds me, there's a bit of whisky left after yesterday's antics.

    sinking into the mattress

and the curtains

    <u>flushed less and less</u>   Don't mean to be funny, but I've never seen curtains blush, or use the toilet, so not sure what you're aiming for here.

the more the sun

    skipped stones

my dirty clothes <u>crawled</u>   I can well believe this, actually.

    towards me

a prostrate bridge to the door

    and lichen clogged

the pores until

    I was no longer singularly

grey

The Museum of Sleeping

Some nights, cold skips through the layers
into your veins, taking a hold of your body
with a metallic certainty.

Other nights, selkies bump against the hull;
there is a known voice calling your name;
you wake up ready to eat.

This night, still well preserved, carries
her, alive, laughing at the waves,
saying nothing at all.

Arran Sequence

1. Machrie Moor

Start on the first page, the scone-
coloured path to the croft's collapsed slates.

Stare under its teeth for a story. One
tree has taken over the walls, fern tentacles

steer through bricks, a chimney of nettles gone
dry; and then, past the loner labels, turn to

stage-struck circles of barnacled bone:
an empty index, a haptic glossary.

Straight-backed bolts in this mix-taped zone,
they've weathered the art of echoes,

storing the years, their surface a drone
of initials and lichen dripped lava-like.

2. The Doon

Above, an absence of fortifications,
shaved to stumps. Deer-shelterers
defended by grenade-shaped shite.

The cliff is a cluster of blades, a face
like a knife. The more the lava
crumbles the sharper it looks.

The sea piles up a collection of marbles:
brain-tinted, a galaxy of mica, yellow-
blooded logs, veined crusts.

Battle lines are covered in moss.

3. Goatfell

Gothic scrabble of rocks, we chat
fey and murder: how this chap fell
gormless or was pushed off his seat.
Few can tell. My shoes have little skill,
goofing off boulders bashed with sky-sweat.
Fern-mouthed, I grapple like a bull
goring a hold where I can in this brat.
Ferry's in the distance, bold as a bell
goading my attempts to keep afloat.
Fedex me your largest and finest hull.

4. The King's Cave

Catered to the imperative,
this church demands quiet
catcalls of wonder, a jive
partnered with the wall's shifting
cards. Here, a knave;
there, a horse too original to
carry credibility. What a dive
this is into a site of
carved myth, no valve
to stop lovers' names from
casing their way in. Prove
which is ancient, which is true.

5. Arran Dawn

so it seems
      not all peaks are
clouds
      this one is obviously
a mountain
      hiding behind a froufrou
of gas
      the next one over
is harder to detect
      steel white-washed
the creeping of gaucheness
      up a slope
the gaudy sky
      is parenting
glue-dipped tinsel
      it's as if stability
has taken a train
      off
the sky
      the road
the signs are
      all up for auction
drying slowly
      but not slowly
enough

6. The Sight

… to her other eye the standing stones
      washed and clothed, she gave him
seemed to prop up those drunks from
      an ointment to see both worlds with
the pub until dawn sobered them up
      but accidentally scratched her eye so
they gave her an aircraft carrier
      that grandness grew holes
but her left eye saw oil eating swimmers alive
      ladders in the walls, ice-gouged floors
the swift swallow of 8,200 tons
      promises vapourising before her eyes

Homecoming, 1999

For Aurélie

We meet again in the park: helmets on turnstiles,
fags put out against the snout of the sprung horse.
You sit on the saddle, cross your fake crocodile
boots. I hunch my back to hide my height.

No paste can hide the constellations on my nose.
Your lips are the colour of a prune past its date.
You roll a joint like a tune, light up, shift weight —
your legs open, a smile playing at your lips.

Your gang joins, dumped into the swings like bin
bags. I scrape the varnish off my nails until
it's a torn-off map.

Terrapin

You spot patterns around
shallow graves — death is stripes,
you say, a regular echo of provocation.

To the ivy you may speak of containment.
Each syllable is a hit in the shell.

You carry your mathematics with you:
a roof, an overturn, a flashing equal sign.

The Museum of Waiting

This first room depicts early versions,
stony with wait.

Crouched over phones,
their gaze remains downwards.
The side that faces the easterly wind
is hairier than the rest.

Most of our collection is safely stored;
we only show you the highlights.
This is our finest possession,
a specimen grown so restless

her insides have crawled outside,
reversing her very fabrication.
Our experts have conducted a careful
biopsy to determine that her eyes

are still very much active, huddled
behind a barrier of nerves,
looking into an unchanging dark.

A Brick Remembers

how it transformed into feathers
for the carnival, finger smudged

whistles, how each recess in the city
smirked rainbows, a cornice

swigged brew, hidden rivers
pressed play and yes, it chafed

at the display, used to being
kneaded and bonded in structure,

but only for a second before
firing into the air.

Azahara [edit]

Azahara (edit | talk | history | links | watch | logs | views) – (View log • Stats)
(*Find sources*: "Azahara" – news • newspapers • books • scholar • JSTOR • free images)

Dubious sources. An upcoming wife who has yet to reach Wikipedia criteria for BLP notability. Kidlant (talk) 13:26, 27 June 2014 (UTC)

- **Delete**: Unsourced stub for concubine. The article is a mess with poor referencing. Bob3k (talk) 15:46, 27 June 2014 (UTC)
- **Delete**: Azahara lacks coverage in independent reliable sources. Furthermore, there is no proof that she inspired the Al madinah Azahara. Lgblue (talk) 16:20, 27 June 2014 (UTC)
- **Keep**: I have received judgements about this article. Now I have to deal with appearances. Nothing about this deletion(s) has had any proof. Her bones have been looted by white space. MichelleMant (talk) 16:50, 27 June 2014 (UTC)
- **Keep**: The ruins have a page. Merge and re-direct? MichelleMant (talk) 18:10, 27 June 2014 (UTC)
- **Delete**: The whole history of the page indicates extensive self-editing and sock-puppetry. London335 (talk) 20:11, 27 June 2014 (UTC)

The Museum of Shared Meals

We have an incredibly diverse collection here,
ranging from the necessity period
to fine examples of competition.

Notice the imp that features in many depictions.

The 'entwined-fork' lace was created to commemorate
the completion of a particularly successful dish.

It is generally assumed that uniform crookery
guarantees success, but research has proven otherwise.

Ys, Ys

Yes, I am the seabirds
washed inside-out, the stained-glass sea,
yawning roofless walls.

Yes, your calls ring straight to voicemails;
you can barely hear my recording
yapping over the waves.

Yes, the proofer has vanished, his
pen unable to underline typos
yet my skin is littered with deaths.

Yes, I timed out and rose in multiples;
each footstep is now visible on the
yellowing floors. I am she, and hers.

Yes, these volumes are unreadable now; it has
always been this way. Only the
young know my tune and it swallows their hearts.

Yes, I lost my last face in the storm; yours
I had eaten after midnight, laughing as

you yelled that the rain was tied in knots.

Yes, I am always laughing. My hands
are falling. I found a bronze bell
yesterday stuck to my back. It gongs.

Yes, I am contaminations,
and you grok this world until
your circuits merge with our paths.

Yes, the couple came to stand next to me; it dictates
that history is an out of sync 'we'.
You wrap it in silk. Present it as a series of gifts.

Yes! Yes! Hear me! The sea boils
purple, steams that we are lies but
Yes! I, she, we, he, they, it can hiss.

Index in Progress

The Monster She Saw

The monster she saw
paddling
across the lawn
thickening with words.

    The monster she saw
    accumulating
    exile/swapping
    our continent for another.

The monster she saw
discoloured
absorbing
the sun.

    The monster she saw
    exposed
    sometimes whole
    sometimes a moment of mine.

Oil on Panel

Richard III

Experts say that the twist
of the spine is no proof
that this villain's unsheathed.

Still, the effect is like knocked
glass to see a play excavated,
pantomime reassembled in bones

emerging
where a crossroad
of cackling tires now ghosts.

Track Changes

High Wycombe, 2nd February 2014

Limestone gags the ring-roads of the soil,
  their secret limits — above it, cars park on the hardboiled
tarmac, not knowing how quickly it'll give out; how quick
  swallowing occurs, even on days easy to decrypt
when you forget that the mines dug for chalk have scrawled
  exclamation marks across the hills, how weather bottled
its feelings for too long and must empty the scrabble bag
  on the board: 'gluttony' joins 'body' to create 'gimcrack';
how, finally, the owner was in the gap between insurance
  policies: footnoted history and an unwritten dance
whose steps are full of earth, a snore of stars and bones
  waiting to recycle her, the car, into correspondence.

Astéronymes

*

In this version of a novel, odd pages
have been turned into plywood bones —
the accordion opens on hands
pointing their asterisk outlines at you.

The names of places you know, The E**** and C****,
The B***** T*******, have been asteronymed.
The places you don't k*** have been asteronymed.
The places that might or might not e**** have been asteronymed.

**

Precision has been given a backstory
to make them more endearing
but it does not excuse their behaviour.

You thought this version of a novel
might make you look at O*****
differently. You thought you might
find gossip about M... R******

and report back to them. You thought
you could object to their depiction
of D***** and the B*******.
You thought their take on P*****
would make for a good status;
what slide consists of 300 comments?

***

Half-way through this version of a novel
you tire of proper names hiding behind
asterisks: where are the atpersands?
the octothorpes? the circumflexes?
Where are the fucking grawlixes
bubbling out like so many oxygen scrawls
from the squares of an Asterix?

To your right, there is a p**.
Resist b********* something you won't stop.
To your left is a l*** interest
it'd be all too e*** to add.
Please forget about the a*****
sitting on your nightstand.

****

Nearing the end of this version of a novel
you are told that the verb has become flesh.

As of January 5th 2015 16.49 UK standard time, I do not give
F******* or any entities associated with F******* permission to
use my p*******, i**********, or p****, both past and future. By this
statement, I give notice to F******* that it is strictly forbidden to
disclose, copy, distribute, or take any other action against me based
on this p****** and/or its contents. The content of this profile is
p****** and c*********** information. The violation of privacy can be
punished by l** (UCC 1-308- 1 1 308-103 and the Rome Statute).

*****

Frankly, the ending of this version of a novel
was a disappointment.
'You will not believe it', so you do.

The most plausible aspect of *Tintin*
is that the Captain wore the same
outfit for several p*a*g*e*s.

Guidebook

After HG Wells' A Short History of the World

i

In my country, we admire distance

Our wild ancestors couldn't hear the world

between the bodies. Men learned

Our wild ancestors made budget guesstimates

to hide our mouths beneath our wings.

Our wild ancestors were keen shoppers

My neighbour has been knitting a scarf

Our wild ancestores lived on milk tokens

for the daughter he thinks I have.

Our wild ancestors did not have 4G

Bulbs are imperfectly settled.

Our wild ancestors had a flair for the dramatic

Historically, we develop

Our wild ancestors worried about their BMI

along similar lines to our brethren,

Our wild ancestors drank less than we do

but with different hairstyles.

Our wild ancestors didn't try to fit in

There are three main kinds of wandering.　Our wild ancestors generally

succeeded

If we were hunters, we would bring honey.　Our wild ancestors detected

movement faster than colour

If we were lost, we would bring skin.　Our wild ancestors are a ROI

It is well to keep the proportion

of things in mind

ii

Geneticists talk of us as being almost human.
Only our objects remain, costume jewellery,
dawn stones. In our braincase we find teeth.
It is unlikely that our tongues could have moved
about for articulate speech. What sort of creature
are we, bat-shaped with cuts upon us like a tally?
Scientific men have named us. No other vestige
like us is known. Yet, the soil is littered with our
implements. We are drawing very near to man.

The Age of Fishes

After HG Wells' A Brief History of the World

It took us a long time to upgrade;
the cause of these changes were very complex.

I moved into your town, so we adapted
to new patterns, swapped alcopops for gin.

Fishes became so prevalent in the rocks
that the city speculated about its walls.

Fishes now gone, fishes allied to today,
fishes pretending to still live yesterday.

Early conditions favoured the development
of every tendency to root and hold on.

The first shells were protections against drying,
the second shells were protections against falling out.

Life was still only in the sea. We moved to land
ever so slowly, learning to dry, learning to fall.

Print of Two Women in a Bar

Artist or Maker: Unknown
Date: 2014? {nd}
Place of Production: Brooklyn? New York, United States of America.
Type of Object: etching on paper, hand-coloured in watercolour and bodycolour.
Accession Number: 4232.7.11.14

Brief description: Satirical print, possibly a book illustration, depicting women and a man playing dominoes and drinking in a bar. In the foreground, to the left, one woman observes a game with a magnifying glass. Her glass of wine is still full. Behind her is a raised table at which one man and a woman are standing playing dominoes. The man has his back turned to us and has no recognizable features. The woman looks directly at us with one hand on her chin as if sizing us up. In the foreground on the right there is a cat, observing the scene. The bar is on the right. The barman is crouching behind the bar, a wisp of smoke suggests a concealed cigarette. There is an overturned stool in front of the bar but no indication of what might have made it fall. The colours are faded with areas of brightness: the content of the glass of wine is vividly red, the woman looking at us has markedly brown hair and eyes. The bar is bottle-green. It is unclear whether these brighter colours were added at a later stage. Around the image there is a border of parallel lines, with an empty plaque below the image. Etched, hand-coloured in watercolour and bodycolour.

The Most Comprehensive Picture

For the Clipperton gang

This world does not behave like billiard balls.
    We are noisy images
harnessed into cooking rotas.
    Our windows shift everyday
from cliffs to sea, to an upturned boat
    with shower facilities.
Steadily, we record our ghost towns,
    buildings conjured from conversations,
streets swimming in wine.
    Some days, the tide runs strongly;
others, we hear three pieces of music
    at the same time,
a sea both too flat and too sharp.
    Approach with caution. Eat it
drenched with colour speckling.

The Museum of Family Portraits

An archive of asylums and dead-ends.
A bad composition confined to the sponge-house.

Building stairs can be fudged
but only in the literal sense.

Climbing out of windows as a standard form of
courtship. See eloping.

Damned and over-married or unmarried and
damned. Either way, awake.

Every night the floor
erupted with nightmares.

For generations, they puckered cogs and bolts into timekeepers on
        a street
filled with other timekeepers.

'Goodnight' is a word she can rarely use.
'Grand jeté' is a word she can often use.

He came back from camp while she was washing her hair.

His deportation was carved in a tobacco tin.

It's just like him to blame a stabbing in a church on a spider.
I have not yet been filed.

"Just imagine if you'd been there with us, André,
just think how you'd laugh at death.

Know that it's taken a holocaust to destroy class.
Know that this carnival won't last."

Like chewing gum on a spring, you
long for the car to splutter to life.

Marriage certificates are littered with kisses.
Many have seeped into the table.

No.
No.

Ought our portrait be bottle-shaped?
Over this sleeve, the varnish is brighter.

Pillaged Cornwall during the pirate years.
Painters taught a Breton lad to swear in English.

Question the origin of the tapestry.
Question the origin of nicknames.

Re: my previous email.
Re: our last century.

She spent a childhood learning to breathe.
Sisters kept widening the family tree.

They boiled and stripped pointe shoes until
they held their bones.

Under the cover of contagion, she lived.
Under the cover of electricity, he lived.

Volumes of maiden names kept like a locket.
Violence in the very butter he spreads.

We have framed his spectacles for safekeeping.
When we rise our eyes hang the same.

X marks the wire.
X litters the letter.

You have been caught in a mousetrap.
You may not pass go.

Lunar Sapphic

To understand astronomy we observe
the following: the smudging of our mirror-
selves, analysis of brand, laying of bets.
The galaxy is

not chipped nail varnish, it's contactless payment,
and we're too analogue to deal with its waves.
The moon smirks at our *hand-folded* thoughts, our *home-
fashioned* predictions...

Variation on the Dissolution of a Biscuit Base

i.

Sad to have disappeared entirely is
reborn go stale I do smell of adventure
I've been grumpy with me. Yes, sorry
am half human. My money is too early.
I do this;   perhaps I'll be great,
will try   to let me.   There's a man
sneezed   behind   the bar
and   then   sat   down

ii

Initials to question

• Put the usage into a word and crush with a multiplicity of concurrent meanings. Stir through the origins evenly.

• Alternatively, use historical phrases to pulse the conditions to a bourgeois society, pour in the industrially advanced and combine social-welfare state.

• Pour the clouded amalgam into inherited language and smooth around with the back of a word. You can use ordinary language to press in the imprint and get an even bureaucratic and mass media jargon.

• Refrigerate for at least half an hour to set the sciences before removing from the traditional categories.

• Release the public from the private by balancing it on public opinion and easing down the precise terms. You can now add your accessibility. Chill again, if necessary, and serve.

iii.

Here I sit bro,
kin-hearted.

The Museum of Bus Stop Queues

Bowling pins holding on to small suns.

Almost all of their work
addresses the theme of retaliation.

They sip time through a straw.

Their book has all the symptoms
of a forgotten ice cream.

'Our main weakness is probably the universe.'

What of their best quality?

They look upstream.

They are always looking upstream.

What Happens in New York

Subjunctive **moods are home**less worlds.
They have neither certainty nor sunsets —
they're not always tethered
to their clause.

> *"The galaxy has billions of them*
> *marked phonetically,*
> *cast away*
> *during the* **chaotic** *birth of their native systems,*
> *they are molten at the core,*
> **but frozen** *at the surface.*
> *There may be oceans of liquid* **judgement** *in the zone*
> *between those extremes.*
>
> *Who knows what might be swimming there?"*

The two most well-known ways of finding
uncertainty rely on wobbles
caused by the gentle **tugs**
of an orbiting pronoun's gravity,
or the slight dimming produced
when a subjunctive passes

between possibility and its star.

> For now, the best methods include
> looking for heat in the infrared.
> We can't easily detect clauseless subjunctives
> that are smaller than a judgement
> or at least 300 times the **mass of doubt.**

Message in a Bottlenose Dolphin*

for Tori

clickclickclickclick
arw
clickclickclickclick
crrrrrreak
clickclickclickclick
arw
clickclickclickclickclickclick
whipewhipe

* Scientists believe that this message is in the fact The Great
Lost Bottlenose Dolphin Poem which was thought to have been
destroyed by the Tiger Shark faction during The Great Dorsal
Insurrection of 210. It is a pioneer of the arion, named after
the dolphin Arion who carried a human poet (which humans,
confusingly, have decided to call Arion) as part of his own
performance. The arion form uses the full range of phonetics with
each line needing to adhere to a particular type. While modern
variations have played with the volume and wavelength of each
utterance, they keep to this general order.

La Vieille

Gorlebella Rock, Brittany, France

I am the bone gatherer
raw rigid rotting reaper
white-waved hair
caught in a fist of rocks.

Hear me clatter my beams
across the velvet rug.

The sea is my mess:
dentures in my wake,
kelp-clothes thrown at the land.

I smell
of freshly-drawn claws
phrased by light.

I rise roaring
or sink
and watch.

Cìr Mhòr

for Alex

LOT 1155

Slate placemats, precariously leaning against each other. Traces of chalk.

LOT 3190

A packet of rose seeds, mixed types, past expiry date.

LOT 1466

A clipping of an obituary, dated September 13 2015. Title: 'Death and resurrection of light'. Obituary begins: *It was an error. As the saying goes, 'rumours of my demise were grossly exaggerated'.*

LOT 2333

A wooden cockerel, salvaged from a fire. The comb is heavily carbonated.

LOT 2334

An incomplete set of dominoes. All the doubles are unaccounted for.

LOT 2455

A letter, dated to March 13 1978. An expert has been able to determine that the blackouts are more recent.

Instructions for Restoring a Friendship

for Helen

Boil until the core separates
from the build-up of years —
check it for damage.

Anything can be repaired.
Anything but this.

I've filled my inbox with salt
to preserve your emails.

They will hold fine.

When we separated, the knives warped
and stopped the drawer from closing.

In the past, I will spend more and be less.
In the future, I am quieter.

The dress you gave me has started a committee.
Your flowers hate me.

I still sing lyrics to the wrong tune,
and imagine you, furiously rescuing
each damaged chorus in your hands
like a small snail.

Spare Me That

'Perhaps I shall not answer you truly in many things that you ask me, concerning the revelations; for perhaps you would constrain me to tell things I have sworn not to utter, and so I should be perjured, and you would not want that.'
Joan of Arc, 24 February 1431, third public examination

When your entire face tingles   *you are about to be tagged*

Domrémy-la-Pucelle's   cookbooks are still radioactive
story is   too dangerous to handle
held captive   by Le Pen

Finding a fire in your belly means   *you must comment*

Lead-lined for 400   years
you've been   costumed at every chance
whatever floats their boat   xenophobia or girl power
hive peg   into a square hole

cemented   in volumes
When no omens manifest   *you must sign in*

Ring the submerged   history
Paint   the walls with disembowelled voices
you   are multiple

Index in Progress (2)

Chikungunya

The island's been set on fire before
exits clotted by price tags,
the weather an incubating belly.

Now it's fevered, houses biting
their neighbours, punctured bricks,
resentment festering in the blood.

Uncomplicated and severe
a language defined
by joints forced into new frontiers.

Tourists, we squinted at an island sutured
over repetition. We are not the neutral.

We darned its skin with thread.
Unstitch, and the sound you'll hear
is air escaping too rapidly.

Item Waiting to Be Catalogued

Mughal painting c. 1635

The last eructation:
a pimpled drake.

We have added a panel of sky
to the drake
in case it is historically important.

Importance is determined by the level
of margarine in its aura, which is quite high.

The absence of gold is not necessarily significant.
The absence of mess suggests it is significant.

NOTES

Several of the poems have been created using a technique I've not found a name for, which involves taking a word, slicing it in two and placing it on either end of the line. The most extreme version of this is probably 'Goatfell' in the Arran Sequence where the mountain has been cut in four as 'Go/at/fe/ll'. Most other poems using this technique give themselves a breather line.

'The Museum of Water'
Created after my 'floating residency' at Amy Sharrocks' exhibition at Somerset House in 2014. Some of the lines have been borrowed from books present at the exhibition.

'Expiry Date'
Inspired by Richard Fortey's *Horseshoe Crabs and Velvet Worms: The Story of the Animals and Plants that Life has Left Behind.*

'Self-Portrait in the Body of a Dolmen'
Inspired by Frances Justine Post's self-portraits in her collection *Beast*, and the dolmens from Quelarn, Plobannalec, Brittany.

'Azahara'
'Azahara' is a fictitious Wikipedia deletion thread for a real person. She was the concubine of the Caliph Abd al-Rahman III and it is

rumoured that the city of Medina Azahara was built for her in 936. The city was forgotten and rediscovered in 1910.

'Ys, Ys'

This poem is inspired by the mythical submerged town of Ys. King Gradlon held the keys to the city doors which, if opened would let the sea in. His daughter Dahut murdered a new lover every night by making them wear a mask that would kill them. Then the devil came to visit, and she fell in love with him, agreeing to steal the keys to the city from her father. As the city was swallowed, Gradlon attempted to save his daughter, but a saint told him to let her go. She became a mermaid.

'Track Changes'

On 2nd February 2014, Zoe Smith discovered that her car had been swallowed by a 30ft sinkhole in her parents' driveway in High Wycombe.

'The Most Comprehensive Picture'

A distilled cento. Lines were stolen from books read by my travelling companions on Fair Isle (where I travelled with the Clipperton Project). Most but not all were taken arbitrarily from p.69. They were whatever they were reading at the time. I then moved away from the cento to include my own words and not all extracts feature in the final version of this poem. For those interested, these were the books:

Nick: *Clyde Cruising Club: Sailing directions and anchorage – Shetland Islands*

Dru: Truman Capote, *Other Voices, Other Rooms*

Jenny: Will Self, *The Book of Dave*

Liz: *The Bible*

Craig: his own song lyrics

Rachel: Maurice Merleau-Ponty, *The Phenomenology of Perception*

John: Brian Cox and Jeff Forshaw, *The Quantum Universe*

Calum: Mark Haddon, *The Curious Incident of the Dog in the Night-Time*

Danielle: Fred Harrison, *Handbook on humanity 1: anatomy of a killing cult*

Mel: William Faulkner, *As I Lay Dying*

Amanda: Bruce Chatwin, *The Songlines*

Dia: Ian Bogost, *Alien Phenomenology*

Molly: Michel de Certeau, *The Practice of Everyday Life*

'The Museum of Family Portraits'

In an abecedarian format, I have collaged pieces of family history and lore. It features, among others: my mother, my great-great-grandfather who died in an asylum, Robert the Bruce, my Trotskyist grandfather who was deported in World War Two, my distant, reputedly piratical, ancestor Jean Coatanlem, and James Hook.

'Variation on the Dissolution of a Biscuit Base'

(i) is based on ClaireBot suggestions on Facebook; (ii) is a Homosyntactical Translation of BBC Good Food's 'How to Make a Biscuit Base' and the introduction to Jürgen Habermas's *The Structural Transformation of the Public Sphere*.

'What Happens in New York'
Base text taken from 'A Guide to Lonely Planets in the Galaxy' by Nadia Drake (*National Geographic*, March 13th 2014) and modified for a Pharmapoetica event in London. Read only the bolded words for a different speed.

'La Vieille'
La Vieille is the name of a lighthouse and translates as 'the crone'.

'Cìr Mhòr'
Poem inspired by Alex Boyd's photograph of Cìr Mhòr on the Isle of Arran, but also Leanne Shapton's *Important Artifacts and Personal Property From the Collection of Lenore Doolan and Harold Morris, Including Books, Street Fashion and Jewelry.*

'Chikungunya'
An infection spread by mosquitos which has had various outbreaks in the last decade, including Guadeloupe, where my father lived.